1,000,000 Books

are available to read at

Forgotten Books

www.ForgottenBooks.com

Read online
Download PDF
Purchase in print

ISBN 978-0-282-59472-5
PIBN 10858283

This book is a reproduction of an important historical work. Forgotten Books uses state-of-the-art technology to digitally reconstruct the work, preserving the original format whilst repairing imperfections present in the aged copy. In rare cases, an imperfection in the original, such as a blemish or missing page, may be replicated in our edition. We do, however, repair the vast majority of imperfections successfully; any imperfections that remain are intentionally left to preserve the state of such historical works.

Forgotten Books is a registered trademark of FB &c Ltd.
Copyright © 2018 FB &c Ltd.
FB &c Ltd, Dalton House, 60 Windsor Avenue, London, SW19 2RR.
Company number 08720141. Registered in England and Wales.

For support please visit www.forgottenbooks.com

1 MONTH OF FREE READING

at

www.ForgottenBooks.com

By purchasing this book you are eligible for one month membership to ForgottenBooks.com, giving you unlimited access to our entire collection of over 1,000,000 titles via our web site and mobile apps.

To claim your free month visit:
www.forgottenbooks.com/free858283

* Offer is valid for 45 days from date of purchase. Terms and conditions apply.

English
Français
Deutsche
Italiano
Español
Português

www.forgottenbooks.com

Mythology Photography **Fiction** Fishing Christianity **Art** Cooking Essays Buddhism Freemasonry Medicine **Biology** Music **Ancient Egypt** Evolution Carpentry Physics Dance Geology **Mathematics** Fitness Shakespeare **Folklore** Yoga Marketing **Confidence** Immortality Biographies Poetry **Psychology** Witchcraft Electronics Chemistry History **Law** Accounting **Philosophy** Anthropology Alchemy Drama Quantum Mechanics Atheism Sexual Health **Ancient History Entrepreneurship** Languages Sport Paleontology Needlework Islam **Metaphysics** Investment Archaeology Parenting Statistics Criminology **Motivational**

A MAKER OF NEW JAPAN.

MARQUIS ITO'S EXPERIENCE

TRANSLATED

BY

Teizo Kuramata,

Late Professor of Nagasaki Commercial School, Author of "A Guide to English Composition," the "Questions and Answers on English Grammar," Etc.

NEW EDITION.

THE

Gwaikokugo Kyojusho,

No. 25, Uma-machi, Nagasaki, Japan.

COPYRIGHTED, 1904 BY
TEIZO KURAMATA.

π—580.5
π 580.5

Bancroft gift

MARQUIS H. ITO.

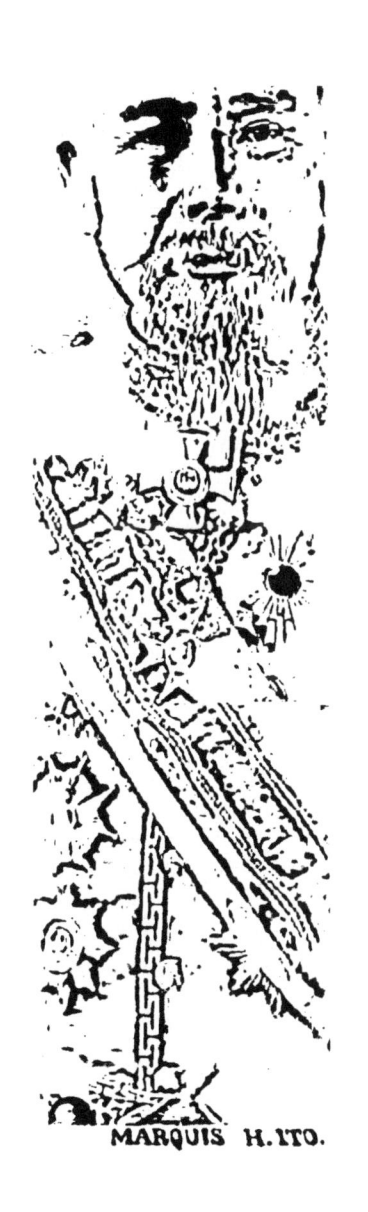

T. KURAMATA.

PREFACE.

I have read the following manuscript, "Marquis Ito's Experience," and found it very interesting, worthy of the eminent person, who has so signally and satisfactorily rendered to his country the great services therein narrated.

Charles B. Harris.

Nagasaki, April 2nd, 1904.

the present Constitution that was sanctioned by the Emperor. Much of his work is worthy to be recorded forever in history. In reflecting upon the fact that Japan has attained her present position under the kind influence of both England and America, and especially that the study of the Constitution of England, which is called "the mother of all constitutions in the world," has greatly helped us in bringing about the elements of New Japan, I dare say that the present work of Mr. T. Kuramata is well fitted to the times.

In concluding this introduction, I express my earnest hope that the present work will be read by the reading public in general, who understand the tongue of our allied country, so that it may furnish good material for those who would study the history of our system.

YUKIMATSU OTA,
Editor of the "Kyushu Hinode."
Nagasaki, April, 1904.

PREFACE.

The Soul of Japan is well compared to a cherry blossom, which opening in the early morning receives the first and purest dew, and so presents, by virtue of the excellence of its beginning, the brightest and most lovely aspect.

As the cherry blossoms open their petals so widely to the brightest sunbeams, so the Japanese people of good culture are eager to receive any foreign civilization that may appear good to them. Being blessed with excellent discrimination they would receive anything new, which they see to be beneficial and right, which they assimilate themselves, and then put to the test. dare say this faculty of assimilation, that i to say Bushido, has helped to make th present Japan, that now ranks as one of th Powers.

Marquis Ito was born at the age wher Bushido, the Soul of Japan, had its ow days, and was fully endowed with goo knightly virtues. As far as my imaginatio goes, he is an incarnation of Bushido, be cause each and every act of his, throug his public career, has proved him to be suc! the noblest dictum of Bushido being alway his Compass to float the ship of the State.

Just as the cherry blossoms receive tl the purest light and dews in the mornin he often flew away to foreign lands in order to imbibe the essence of the flowery civilization there, in the dawn of the present era. Discarding all his prejudices there, and being heavily laden with valuable information instead, he flew back home. Thus he has enriched his hive, the community in general. Yes, he has rendered many valuable services to the Emperor and the country, and consequently has done his ample share in making Japan the most noticeable country in the Far East, and attracts attention as much as the most beautiful flower which has imbibed the purest light and crystal dews arrests our eyes. So I think the title "a maker of New Japan" is well fitted to his honour, because he was mainly instrumental in drawing up the present Constitution.

The strong belief that I am second to none in worshipping Bushido has induced me to translate his own account of his experiences in the hope of letting foreigners know of his character as well as well his loyalty as a living exponent of our Bushido.

In concluding this preface, I wish to express my hearty thanks for many valuable suggestions, with which A.E. Rigby, B.A., Professor of Chinzei Seminary, has kindly enriched the present work.

TEIZO KURAMATA.

Nagasaki, March 25th, 1904.

A MAKER OF NEW JAPAN.

MARQUIS ITO'S EXPERIENCE.

The following is the story related by the Marquis himself in compliance with the urgent request of the late Otowa, one of the famous novelists of modern Japan:—

Well, I will relate what I experienced in attempting the first tour through Europe. Whenever I recall the past, it seems to me as if I am now existing in another world. I say that the students of to-day are a thousand times blessed in every respect, because at the time of our student life, we had no better ships than a few sailing *boats* for going abroad; and consequently there were very few who would go abroad, but at present those who go across the ocean can clothe themselves in foreign attire in their native places, and have splendid ships for traveling in. What an enviable condition of affairs it is, when compared with the epoch of our student life! And, moreover, important scientific and literary works in abundance are imported; and an endless variety of translations are published, so that they can study any subject they like. We had only an English dictionary translated by Tatsunosuke Hori, before we went abroad. As there were very few who could understand English well at that time, many mistakes naturally found their way into this rare and costly book. This dictionary and a series of the Nippon

Seiki, "Political History of Japan," by Sanyo Rai were the only books we took with us to foreign lands.

It was in the year of the Bunkyu era (1862), thirty seven years ago, that I sailed on a foreign tour. Before this I was in Kyoto, having left Yedo (the present Imperial Capital). I remember that the debates and discussions then excited the whole nation; they were much louder than the debates held in the present Diet, or the discussions engaged in by the politicians of to-day. There were two parties of politicians at that time. The object of one was to carry out the principle of seclusion, while that of the other was to open up the country to trade. The former was stronger than the latter, and those who belonged to the former party cried out "expel the barbarians," and the plan for successfully carrying out their end was simply to defend the country with guns, laying the same along the whole sea-coast of Japan, as the material for these guns was to be obtained from the hanging bells of all the temples of Japan. Such being their rough idea, they were going to drive out all foreigners. So there were very few who dared venture to express themselves in favor of opening up the country, for fear they would be murdered for so doing. Therefore those who tried to create sentiment in favor of opening up the land did so at the cost of their fortunes and lives, for their country's sake.

I was living in Kyoto, the former Imperial Capital, just when the feeling towards expelling foreigners reached its climax. In the same year, or the year before, though I do not exactly remember which, the Shogun Iyeshige paid a visit to the August Master's court, in order that he might obtain the Imperial sanction regarding that measure. So the rumour got abroad that the Imperial Edict would be published, while the Shogun was staying in the Imperial city. In the meantime a few friends who were willing to go abroad with me were fortunately found. To mention their names, they were Kaworu Inouye still living, the late Masaru Inouye of the Rai'way Office, the late Yozo Yamane, and the late Kinsuke Endo of the Coinage Office, so we were five altogether. But in attempting to take voyage, there arose a difficulty, for I sulted Genzui Kusaka about the ma He died afterwads at the time of the turbance which broke out in Kyoto. I a member of his party whose principle to expel all foreigners at any cost. I told by him that it was too late for m attempt going abroad, owing to the ur existing in the country. There was no cessity of consulting anybody else, as it obvious that I should be hindered a from going abroad, if I asked advice f others. But I was trying my best accomplish my desire. I was not at disappointed, for Inouye and others eager to take me to Europe with th

When I was ordered to go up to Tokyo, formerly Yedo, by my Daimyo, they came after me and prevailed upon me to prepare for the trip. So it was decided that we should arrange every thing for it. But, sad to say, I was something like an absconder, having had no permission to go abroad, while the four others had obtained private orders to go from the Daimyo of the Choshu clan. As it was then strictly forbidden by the Tokugawa Regency for any one to go abroad, it was necessary for us to disguise ourselves as merchants, and not to wear our two swords. At that time Zoroku Murata, one of the famous Dutch teachers, who was afterwards known as Zoroku Omura, was living in the Choshu clan quarter of Tokyo. He was then teaching Dutch in that quarter, but after the restoration of the "Imperial Power" he was appointed Captain. When I paid him a visit, he showed me great sympathy, saying that we had better go out of the country as soon as possible. After a while I left him asking him to do his best for my sake, and when I left the country I left a note addressed to him.

As we were then obliged to take a foreign steamer, we had, of course, to apply to a fereign shipping company near the Custom House. There was then one known among Japanese as "English No. 1 Firm" in Yokohama. As I was acquainted with the manager and employees, and as there was a gentleman, by the name of Girl, in that office, who could speak Japanese very well; I applied directly to him for our tickets as soon as I could. Our application being readily granted, we got our 6000 *ryo* changed for dollars, through him. Thus we had $ 8000, most of which we again had changed for Bills of Exchange, through him also. The money which we kept in our pockets was very little, but enough to defray all the petty expenses which the journey necessitated. Mr. Kayemon Takashima, who is still living, lived at that time on the Kanagawa Hill. Under his residence there was a tea-house called "Shimodaya" whose proprietor was a servant of the Choshu clan. As all travellers who came from the clan used to rest there, we also went there to rest, and thoroughly transformed ourselves into merchants, leaving off our two swords. Thus entering the town, we put up at a hotel. In the meantime we had often gone out shopping into the foreign concession. To tell the truth, the settlement was not so prosperous as it it is now, there being only a few foreign houses scattered here and there. Though we had to clothe ourselves in European style, yet we could not get any new suits of clothes ready made, but only second-hand ones, such as are demanded by sailors only, and we could not find any better boots than those of such a size that into one we could put both our feet at once. Against our will, we were obliged to take those above mentioned, owing to the smallness of the stock in the store. Then, as we had not yet our hair dressed in European style, no wonder we appeared quite strange, both to Europeans and natives, when we wore foreign clothes and boots. As a steamer was then sailing from Yokohama to Shanghai, we were told that we should come to the firm in question in the middle of that night, so that we might be taken on board the vessel by the Captain, after he had taken his meal. The firm in question is still in existence in Yokohama. The building was then surrounded by a fence, inside of which there was a small hill to which we were directed to come, and wait. While we were waiting there for the Captain we managed to get our hair cut in European style. Although our physicians of that time had their queue cut off, I may safely say that we set the first example to the nation for dressing the hair in European style. It gave us a very strange feeling when we touched our heads, and at the same time we felt very much embarrased when anybody looked at us. As it was drawing near twelve o'clock, the English gentleman, by name Girl, came out of his room to meet us there, and directly gave us a flat refusal, saying that it was quite unlawful for him to take us out of the country from which people were strictly forbidden to go by the Tokugawa Regency.

He added that he could not guarantee whether or not he could safely get passage for us. Then I was greatly disappointed, and said; "If so, we are ruined and disgraced, so much so that we have no alternative, but to kill ourselves here; because if we go home with this semi-foreign appearance we shall certainly be killed as spies. So we had better die at this moment than be brought up to the court, making a sorry, crestfallen picture, to be sentenced to death." Just at the moment when all of us were going to lay our hands on our swords, the Englishman in question was much terrified, and said, " Do not go to such an extreme as killing yourselves, but wait a moment while I go back to my partners and have another consultation over the matter." To our great relief, we were immediately told that we could go. It was just two o'clock in the morning, when silence reigned over the surrounding country, that the Captain went forth first and then Mr. Girl took us on board with him. On the way to the ship we were told by Mr. Girl that we should talk louder, while he would say something unintelligible to the Customs officials, when we had to pass in front of the Custom House. So we did as we were told, and reached the pier where we found a sampan waiting for us, in which we were taken to the steamer. In the ship were a few Customs officials; so, for ar of being caught by them we were hidden in the engine room, until the ship set sail. Soon after daybreak, when we saw "Cape Kwannon" on the coast, we were allowed to go on deck, to our relief. The weather, however, being bad during the trip from Yokohama to Shanghai, we scarcely took food on that short voyage.

After landing at Shanghai, we took a walk through the town. The foreign concession appeared fine and clean to us. As nobody but Masaru Inouye of the Railway Office could speak intelligible English, we asked through him how we should be taken from here to Europe, and were told that we must wait there, until there was another steamer sailing for Europe. And after a while, we were transferred to the store-boat which was used as a kind of warehouse, an[chored] in the harbour for storing cargo[es] of opium. As long as we stayed there w[e] were badly treated. We could take noth[-]ing but bread and the leavings on the plate[s] of others, on which dogs are fed. So w[e] were all miserable, but sometimes we were in[-]vited to dinner by an Englishman, by nam[e] Keswick, who was then an agent for th[e] firm before mentioned. The dinners give[n] us by him were not elaborate, but taste[d] very good, as we were accustomed to livin[g] on poor food. To do him justice, he wa[s] a very kind fellow, and gave us each som[e] English books, and on seeing our impatienc[e] he sometimes comforted us by saying tha[t] we would be taken to Europe very soo[n]

To tell the truth, we were all looked upon as children by him, to our regret; though I was twenty three years old, by the lunar calender, Kaworu Inouye was twenty nine, Masaru Inouye was a year or two younger than I, and Endo and Yamane were a few years older than I. He could not realize that we had occupied ourselves in discussions and debates upon politics in Japan. But it could not be helped, because we could not fully express our thoughts in English·

There was a merchant vessel sailing for Europe, having tea as cargo; her displacement tonnage being about one thousand four or five hundred, and her length being three hundred feet. To this sailing boat Kaworu Inouye and I were taken.

The other three came, a week later,
another ship. The ship we (Kaworu Inou
and I) took being a very poor kind
vessel, we were taken into a small cab
near the sailors' quarters at stern. As o
quarters were poor'y furnished, we we
indeed miserable. And moreover we we
badly treated, so much so that we could n
take our meals until all of the passang
had finished theirs, although we did n
of course, sit at the same table with t
sailors. I had a strong belief th
they thought we intended to beco
sailors, because they sometimes forced
to work with them in adjusting the r
gings, if it rained on a sudden, or if th
wanted a few extra hands. When

slept too late in the morning, they came into our room and awoke us by striking us with the end of ropes, saying "Japs, get up, get up." Thus we experienced many hardships on the passage. As the Suez Canal was not then opened, we were obliged to sail round the Cape of Good Hope, without touching at any harbour after leaving Shanghai. At last we arrived in the dock at London, having spent four months in this voyage. As we sailed along the coast, we could see distinctly the outline of the Cape of Good Hope, also St. Helena, to which isle Napoleon the First was banished. But on account both of the expense, and of the long time which we should spend by so doing, we did not touch at any of the historical places, to our regret. The most trying experience, which we had on the passage, was the scarcity of drinking water, which was supplied by catching rain in large pails which were set on the deck; so that when fine weather continued for many days, we were indeed very badly off, being altogether at the mercy of the weather. Regarding our food, we took nothing but hard, dry biscuits, and some salt beef, which was cut into slices of square form, and bean soup which was a most delicious dish to us. As it was often said among some of the passengers that it was necessary to acquire the English tongue first of all, by pains-taking study, and with the *help of an* English- Japanese Dictionary by

Tatsunosuke Hori, we at last found ourselves easily understood by foreigners when we asked for cold water, hot water and so forth, before we arrived in London.

As soon as we had safely entered the dock at London, some Customs officials came on board to examine our luggage, from the largest down to the smallest package. After all of the passengers had landed, the ship underwent strict examination by the Customs officials, called searchers, it being suspected that some contraband goods might be hidden somewhere. On that morning Inouye first landed with a stoker, and I was left alone in the ship In the meanwhile I was getting hungry and thirsty, but could get nothing, because no one was there except the grave looking Customs officials. I did not dare to ask them to get me something to eat and drink. When the evening shades fell I was indeed badly off, but Inouye had not yet come back. An Englishman, who was once a Captain of a steamer owned by the "English No. 1 Firm" Yokohama came on board to guide me to the town, and I was very glad to follow him to a place called the Tower of London and to put up at a hotel in American Square, where seamen used to resort. The next morning I was taken by him to a barber's, a tailor's, and a shoe-maker's. After that I appeared like a gentleman. The clerk of the firm in question took me to many professors', asking each to let me stay at his house and to give me instruction in English, but his request was not granted by any of them, until he and I came round to see Dr. Williamson, Professor of the London University then lecturing in the Chemistry College, who kindly granted his request on my behalf. The reason was this, that no Japanese student had ever been to London before us; so that they found it very strange to instruct me. Inouye and Yamao were under the care of a painter. Dr and Mrs. Williamson daily and nightly instructed me in the language, and in mathematics at their leisure, while I helped the Professor in the school laboratory. To tell the truth, I was not soon able to read the London Times, though I was kindly taught both to read and write. One day a member of the family who was reading a paper, askead me where my native place was. "Choshu" being my answer, he asked again whether Choshu was not the same as Shimonoseki, where a foriegn ship was fired at by the natives. Being surprised to hear of the event I borrowed the paper and asked Masaru Inouye to read it to me. He read that the Parliament was discussing the question of sending an expedition to chastize the Coshu clan. Before this I had been shown into the observatory at the Kew Gardens, the arsenal at Greenwhich, a few ship-building yards, and several other important buildings, spending many Sundays, so the greatness of *England* was thus vividly brought before my mind. Therefore, at this event, I thought that the Choshu clan was blindly planning to fight with such a powerful country as England, without considering fully the probable danger. It was quite plain that the Choshu clan would lose the day, should such a war begin, and consequently the country would be ruined. Thereupon Kaworu Inouye and I thought that it was not necessary for us to continue our studies in England, while our country was endangered. So we made up our minds to go back home at once, in order that we might be instrumental in dissuading the Choshu clan government from carrying out the principle of seclusion, even at the cost of our lives. But though we were obliged to stop our studies when but half completed, we advised the other three to stay there and pursue their studies, according to the original plan. On hearing their promise that they would surely do so, we parted from them.

On my taking leave of Professor Williamson I was kindly told by him that I ought to stay with him a little longer, in order to prosecute my studies, as it was impossible for us to secure a peaceful settlement of the controversy, since we were too young for such a heavy task. But, on my saying that nothing could prevent me from carrying out my desire of going home, the Professor at once yielded to me, and accordingly he got passage for us back home. We were again obliged to sail round the Cape of Good Hope, spending a longer time than we had expected. It was at the beginning of the next year (1863) that we arrived at Shanghai. As I was then able to converse fairly in English, I was told by one of the passengers that a fleet would arrive at Bakwan (Shimonoseki) in a few days, which would be too late for us. But I answered that we should return home any way, no matter whether we were too late or not. As the ship did not then touch at Nagasaki, we landed at Yokohama. On entering Yedo we were greatly surprised to see that the clan official residence was burnt down, and to learn that the Choshu men were all banished from their quarter in the Capital. At that time the ill-fated Choshu men found it very hard to travel through the country.

Inouye and I had been consulting about the matter while on board, and as the result of our consultations we determined to meet Jiozan Sakuma of Shinano province, whose foresight was then known throughout Japan, in order that we might be guided by his profound experience. When we landed at Yokohama we put up at a hotel, where foreigners used to resort, for fear our lives would be endangered, in case it should be known that we were just landing from a foreign vessel. I remember that the man who took us to the hotel was one Harrison, with whom we were acquainted in connection with the "English No. 1 Firm." Through his advice we represented ourselves as Portuguese; my adopted name was Deporner. Inouye's I have now forgotten. At the hotel we deliberated over what road we should take to our clan, but without result. We could not get home by land, while we had no opportunity to return by sea, though we had enough money to do so. Then a rumour got abroad that the men-of-war of several Powers were sailing for Shimonoseki, in a few days, for the purpose of bombardment. We were further informed that the fleet consisted of eighteen ships, so we lost no time in proceeding to the British Legation at Yokohama, and on seeing Her Britanic Majesty's Minister we said, "Sir, we were sent to Europe by our Prince, but on hearing that a war was going to break out between the Powers and Japan we have come back in order to try to bring the flict to an amicable settlement Would be good enough to escort us to the Cho clan?" As there were then a few foreig who could speak Japanese well, such Wallcock, Her Britanic Majesty's Minis Mr. (now Sir) Ernest Satow, Seaport, Lawder, it was not difficult to have application understood by them Howev our request was not readily granted on ground that we were quite incapable successfully interfering in this matter, that the powers were ready to fight at moment. Not being discouraged by refusal, we importunately asked the Bri Minister to grant our request on our affi ing that we could easily dissuade our from going to such an extreme as trying to expel foreigners. Then he said that he would have a consultation on the matter with the respective Ministers of France, America, and Holland, before he could answer our request. After a while the British Minister instructed us to attend the meeting to be held with the respective Ministers, the English Admiral and the French Admiral, which we did. At the meeting we were told that we should be safely escorted by men-of-war, and were asked where our destination was, to which question we replied that we desired to be taken to Himeji in Bango province, because it was very dangerous to get near the coast of Choshu province, owing to the apprehension that the natives there would attack our ships. This request being unanimously granted, we were asked again when we would be able to report to them the ersult of the advice given by us to the authorities of our clan. We answered that we would do so in two weeks from that day, because we wanted to go to Yamaguchi from Himeji, and to return to the latter place after conferences had been held at the former. But they said that they could not wait any longer than twelve days. Having agreed with them regarding the time, we were taken to Himeji, being escorted by British and a French men-of-war. I remember that Satow accompanied us to our destination. On arriving at Himeji we hired a fishing boat to take us to Toun a landing place in Suwo province near Mitajiri.

On landing there we were surprised to see great excitement prevailing throughout our clan, the purpose of expelling foreigners reached its focus, so that women, as well as men, were ready to fight at any moment, being powerfully armed with long lances, and dressed in a way to make their movements easy, and having white cloth bandages round their heads, with their sleeves crisped up to their shoulders by strings called "Tasuki'' in Japanese. We wore the summer clothes which we bought at Yokohama, but we had neither "Hakama" (trousers used for ceremonial occasions) nor two swords, and our hair was still dressed in foreign style, which

was a disadvantage upon entering th
Fortunately a friend of mine, by
Hyoma Yugawa, was then Gover
Mitajiri, two miles from Toumi.
no time in proceeding to his re
and asked him to help us to travel s
Yamaguchi, in an express palanquin
we had to arrive very quickly. Our
being granted, we transformed oursel
" Samurai" through his kind g
"hakama," "hawori" (coats), and othe
garments, and two swords. As it w
strictly forbidden for any one to en
town of Yamaguchi without passpor
Governor in question also gave u
papers. Every sekisho (barrier) was
up; because the Choshu clan wa

actively engaged against the Tokugawa Regency, in order that they might carry out their purpose of expelling foreigners, and so the clan was keeping strict watch for spies. Towards evening we arrived at Yamaguchi and put up at a hotel, and the next morning I met one Mori, a friend of mine, who was serving in the Daimyo's retinue, and asked him to let us see the Daimyo personally, even if we should be killed in front of the Master. Then he said, "I fully sympathize with your loyal spirit in coming back home on hearing of the unrest of our province. Be assured that I will manage to let you have the pleasure of seeing your Master." We heartily thanked him, and retired to our hotel at once.

The next day we were called up to official residence of our Daimyo, and t? in the presence of the Daimyo and ministers we spoke for nearly four h about the greatness of European civilizat as we thought at the time it was advis to do so. We had taken a map with which helped us a great deal in telling the experience we got in Europe. further we related what we had seen of size and construction, as well as the ar ment of the eighteen warships, which anchored in the Yokohama harbour, the intention of bombarding Shimonc in a few days, and showed the hopeless of the resistance against them; for only *Mori* family was prepared to engage in active resistance, while other clans would not unite with his clan. We then retired from the presence of our Master, after having fully expressed our opinion that we, the Choshu clan, should make peace with the Powers. At the same time, we shou'd try our best to restore the Imperial power rather than pursue such a bold, because less wise, policy against such odds. By so doing Japan might have one able central government instead of a feaudal system which only rendered the government unable to withstand the demands of the foreign Powers. Before we left Yokohama the respective Ministers had asked us to take a letter written by then to Prince Moji, our Daimyo, and we promised to do so. However, the circumstances did not make it seem wise to keep promise, because we did not know what it contained, and we also entertained some fears that we might be suspected, by our prince, of being spies for foreigners. To tell the truth, we kept that letter in our hands, even though it was an improper and illegal act. If I am not greatly mistaken, the contents were as follows; " We regret to acknowledge that the Choshu clan has become the common enemy of the world, on account of its forming a confederation of Western Japan against our respective Powers, that have already entered into amity with the Emperor, and its acting against law and order in firing at our ships without cause.

In consequence of this we, the respective Powers, could not but chastize the common enemy, and we are going to send our fleet with the intention of bombarding. In the meanwhile the two young students who were sent to Europe by your Highness's private orders have just returned for the purpose of saving their country from danger, and applied to us to send them to their home, so we have gladly consented to do so. So you see, our real desire is not to fight. We earnestly hope that you will take the matter into consideration and propose a complete friendly understanding. But, if your determination is to fight with us, at any cost, it would be quite necessary for us to rely upon bombardment. In the event of our

taking this measure, we would certa[in]
push our way into the Imperial Palace a[nd]
which we would try to open the country
trade, under His Majesty's sanction, as [the]
united forces of England and France h[ad]
already done in Peking." Though I [did]
not show the original to the Prince, I sp[oke]
of the general tenor of it. Being a l[ong]
long time since we had last seen the Pr[ince,]
we could not part from him easily, [but]
fondly remained beside him. As the c[on]-
ference was not at once settled, we reti[red]
to our hotel. Not being able to tell [our]
fate, we decided to return to our na[tive]
places, in order to see our parents be[fore]
danger beset us. Inouye's native place [was]
Yamaguchi, but mine was Hagi. So

went home to take leave of our parents, then living, and awaited the result of our hazardous adventure.

In the meanwhile the debates and discussions of the clan had begun to take another direction. The Daimyo's guards had a suspicion that Inouye and I were responsible for the change of policy on the part of the clan, so they determined to assassinate us. Being much surprised, Inouye said, " As we have returned from Europe for the purpose of aiding in an amicable settlement of affairs, and now find our lives in danger, it would be better for us to kill ourselves rather than to die at the hands of assassins."

I replied, " Under the existing circumstances we shall surely die, so it will be better for us to await the assassins if they will come to-night, and abide by the result, than to kill ourselves now." Fortunately we were not driven to this extreme, as the Clan Government forbade any violence against us. At that time there was another party called Kiheitai whose object was to expel foreigners from Japan. The leader of this party was one Takasugi, and he had an assistant one Yamagata, now Marquis Yamagata. When we had just returned from Europe, we found that Mr. Takasugi had been imprisoned on account of an illegal act against the Choshu government, but he was released, and set at large by the same government, of which he eventually became an official. The soldiers of this party called on us and said that, as we had once been members of their party, our lives should be guarded and kept safe. I think such sympathetic consideration may be found in both parties, such as the progressive and the liberal.

The day appointed by the respective Powers, was near at hand. In the meantime there were many dangers which we encountered, but I cannot dilate upon them all, only having time and space to give a general view of them. As the men-of-war were waiting for our answer, we had many consultations with the officials of the Government but no result. On account of there being but a few days left, a meeting was held at the Assembly Hall of the Clan

Government. As a result of this mee[ting]
it was decided to send the following ans[wer:]
" The Choshu Clan did not voluntarily [carry]
out the policy of expulsion of foreig[ners,]
but acted under the orders of the Imp[erial]
Government, and therefore it is nece[ssary]
that Prince Mori representing the whol[e clan]
should proceed to the Imperial Capital [in]
order to interview personally the men
of His Majesty's Government, after w[hich]
interview the clan will give a definite r[eply.]
As it will, however, take some conside[rable]
time to effect this, we hope you will [post]
pone the date for the receipt of our a[nswer]
for a period of three months. Should [this]
request not be granted by you, we [must]
inform you that we shall be quite pre[pared]

for hostilities." Inouye objected to such a very unsatisfactory answer being sent, but I said it was better to send such a reply than none at all. We therefore decided to take this message to the frigate, and therefore we took a boat from Mitajiri to Himeji. We arrived at Himeji on the evening of the appointed day. When we met Mr. Satow on board the ship, he said, "I am very glad to see you back! We did not expect to see you again. Let us drink each other's health in some champagne." Mr. Satow forced us to accept at once, and to give him an answer quickly, so we said we had tried our best to settle the matter amicably, but without result. He then asked us if we had given the letter to the Prince, or had brought an acknowledgement of it, and we replied in vague terms. But at length we told him that if he pressed us for an answer we could only give it at the cost of our lives. On our parting from him he said, "Let us meet again under the shower of bullets."

We then returned home, where, to our great surprise, we learned that Prince Mori was going up to Kyoto with Prince Sanjo and seven other "Kuge" (court nobles). There were already in the Imperial city Fukuhara, Masuda, Kunitsukasa, Kido, and others, whose intention was to commence hostilities. Though it was publicly announced that this party was proceeding to the Imperial city for the purpose of apologizing to their August Master for their wrongful acts and intentions against the foreigners, the real reason of their going was to make preparations for offensive demonstrations.

I wish here to mention one Seitaro Shimidzu, a descendant of Chozaemon Shimidzu who killed himself at the sieze of the Takamatsu Castle, on account of thirst arising from the scarcity of pure water. When we called on him one day he urgently pressed us to give him our opinions, regarding the existing condition of affairs, which we did. This gentleman, being as just and honourable man as Takakage Kohayagawa, said, " Your opinion is very just, and I agree with you with all my heart, I will restrain my desire for the expulsion of foreigners for fifty years from this date. therefore request that you will go up t Kyoto as soon as possible, and endeavour t put a stop to the measures taken by ou men, while you try to aid in the restoratio of the Imperial power." We replied in th affirmative, and while we were coming t Okayama, in the Bingo province, we m defeated soldiers who were staggering alon the road. These soldiers had fought a Kyoto. At Okayama we learned that Prin Sanjo and seven other court nobles h retired to Muromotsu, in the province Harima, by sea; so we were obliged to r turn to Mitajiri, and there we met t Daimyo and a meeting was held in l presence. "We lost the day at Kyoto, a in consequence all the Choshu men have been so discouraged that it has been found almost out of the question to fight another battle at Bikwan, against the foreign men-of-war," was the general cry in that meeting. Then "what are the best means of satisfactorily arranging matters with the Powers" became the question. I replied, "It is very difficult at present to arrange matters, but we will try our best." As it was difficult to sail for Yokohama, we were obliged to sail via Nagasaki. In these negotiations we spent a few days uselessly, then we heard that the 18 men-of-war had arrived at Himeji. That night we put up at a hotel in Yamaguchi. A prisoner, by name Masanosuke Shufu, was then set free and restored to his former office. In a conference, that man asked my opinion regarding the condition of affairs, and I expressed it as my opinion that the matter might be satisfactorily settled by our ceding a coaling and watering station to the Powers as well as securing to them the convenience of getting provisions in Shimonoseki, though the Powers might be determined to fight over the matter. This opinion being accepted by him, it was decided that a letter should be despatched by our Prince to the Powers, but having no time to consult with others regarding the writing of such a letter, we wrote it ourselves, and then took it to the Prince's bed-room, and asked him to sign it. We had given orders to one Kozo

Matsushima, of Mitajiri, w' o was then called the Admiral of our fleet, to be ready to accompany us, and the next morning we arrived at Mitajiri, and had to pull in an open fishing boat for 14 or 16 miles to Himeji. When we were half way there, we saw a steamer going to Shimonoseki, so we thought that it was too late for us to put an end to hostilities. That night we stopped at Mitajiri, and the next morning we came back to Yamaguchi.

Takasugi, who had been imprisoned in his own room, was then released and set at large. When we had just returned from Europe, we thought that necessary to let Takasugi know of our opinions, so Inouye had an interview with him at Hagi, before he was released. The interview turned out to be instrumental in drawing him to our party. When I met him he said to me, "It is very awkward to be called to the presence of our Daimyo, without receiving any notice of my being set at large. At any rate, as it is useless to spend many days here, let us go to Bakwan at once. So at two o'clock that afternoon we started for Bakwan by palanquin, where Inouye had already gone. When we got near Kogori about four miles distant from Yamaguchi, the sound of bombarding was heard from the direction of Bakwan. About ten o'clock we met men covered with white bandages around their heads, and armed with weapons, who were coming towards us in palanquins. On questioning them we were told that they belonged to Choshu and were making their way to Yamaguchi for the purpose of informing our Daimyo of the fact that hostilities had begun. On meeting with another palanquin after a while, we asked who was in it, and were told that Inouye was just coming back to Yamaguchi from Bakwan. So we three had our conveyances placed on the ground, and began a consultation. Inouye spoke first, " Though I have been at Bakwan, yet all negotiations have ended in failure. I met Satow on board the man-of-war, but he said that he would present us with bullets this time, and so hostilities began that evening. I returned via Dannoura and saw that the bullets of the " Armstrong " fell short, to our relief. I think, however, we must try not to make our clan stop hostilities, as it is quite advisable to let them know how very impossible it would be to continue hostilities against the Powers. Now let us three go back to Yamaguchi and advise our Prince to go out to the men of Choshu and Suwo." His proposal was at last accepted as the result of a meeting held in the presence of our Daimyo. The next day our Prince set out for Kogori. Inouye was given the charge of defending the place, as it was the most important route to Yamaguchi.

Takasugi and I were given the charge of defending Bakwan. On our arriving at *Kiyosuye*, we were sent back to Yamaguchi by the Prince on urgent business, and when we returned to Kogori we were informed that the Prince was inclined to adopt peaceful measures, and we three were ordered to take charge of all negotiations tending towards peace. The Prince said, "We have carried out our plans to this point, but now we are compelled to ask for an armistice, as our experience goes." Takasugi, who was utterly disatisfied with the treatment he had received at the hands of the Prince, said, "I cannot agree with your Highness's opinion at this moment, since we have commenced hostilities, and should carry out our original plan." The Prince angrily replied, "You don't listen to your Master's commands." Then Takasugi replied that he did not mean to disobey, for if he refused to listen to his Master it would be better for him to commit "harakiri" there in the presence of the Prince. It was unanimously decided that negotiations for a peaceful settlement should be entered upon at once. The Prince's retinue was therefore dispatched, with the necessary orders, to all the commanders of the troops, and when they returned we were to go to the men-of-war to ask for an armistice preliminary to negotiating for a peaceful settlement. As the messengers were late in returning, I went on, in an open fishing boat, On getting near the largest of the men-of-war, the "Conquest," of 72 guns, I asked the watch to let me come on board, but he refused, and directed me to the frigate, at which he pointed, to which I accordingly proceeded. On approaching the side of the frigate, Satow, who was on board, recognizing me, came to the side of the vessel and called out, "Are you tired of fighting, Mr. Ito?" I asked him to let me have an interview with the Admiral, to which he replied, "No! He is engaged in giving orders as to how to capture the guns on the coast. But come to my room." When I entered his room I saw Captain Alexander, who had been shot in the leg by our men. Mr. Satow, pointing to him said, "Your men have acted with great violence," and I really felt full of sorrow. The Admiral meanwhile returned to his room where I went and asked him to stop the bombardment. To this the Admiral agreed, and the bombardment was immediately stopped. The Admiral asked me why the Prince had not come to ask for a cessation of hostilities, to which I replied that the Prince was indisposed, and that therefore I had been deputed to represent him in these negotiations. In the meanwhile Takasugi calling himself Shishido Bingo, came to the ship in another open boat, wearing an "eboshi," (a hat generally worn by noblemen), and a "shitatare," (a long garment also worn by noblemen). When I recognized him, on looking through binoculars, I was surprised at this strange appearance. When he came on board and the negotiations were formally opened, he was asked if he had brought credentials from the Prince, to which he replied in the negative. Then the Admiral said that the negotiations were closed until the Prince himself came on board. The Powers wished to make a great many conditions and demands, one being that they must occupy Hikoshima Island, before any negotiations could be opened. I positively refused this condition, and then Takasugi and I returned to the headquarters at Funaki, for the purpose of interviewing the Prince there. The Powers wanted to keep one of us on board as a hostage, so Inouye remained on the vessel. When we returned to headquarters we found several men, about 14 or 15, walking about and discussing something, which struck us as being very strange. At this moment a man, named Magozo Kubo, son of our writing instructor, at that time Governor of Funaki, came up to us and said, "At present these men are considering the question of assassinating you." At that time there were people who were forming a conspiracy against our lives, on account of their resentment at their defeat at Kyoto. I think these men were under the command of Yamada and Shinagawa. Takasugi, being disgusted, said to me, "Curse these fellows. We must not let then kill us at this juncture. We have important business requiring our earnest attention. But even the government cannot aid us in such an emergency, so we had better leave Funaki and go to some distant part of the country."

greed with him, and so we took refuge at a farmer's five or six-miles away, going there by night. Then Governor Kubo gave us all the assistance he could for our escape, and said, " We cannot but recognize with sorrow the existing condition of affairs in our clan. If this condition continues much longer, our province will be ruined." Our Clan Government had heard of our flight, and sent for Inouye at Shimonoseki, so he returned to Funaki. Our Prince and the government officials announced their assurance that our lives would not be endangered. As the Governor knew the place of our refuge, he was sent to us, accompanied by Shishido and Inouye, and accordingly we were forced to return to Funaki. Then we

went to Bakwan with the clan Minister ?
eleven others, and at last came to
amicable agreement.

Before this it is sad to relate the Ka
shima men killed some foreigners at Nar
mugi in Kanagawa, and thus a war
vengeance occurred. On hearing of (
sad event both Satsuma and Choshu n
became more vigilant. At that time
general opinion of the people of Japan co
not be reached, and even at the Imper
Court no debates resulted in any satisfact
end. The Tokugawa Regency decided
open the country to trade, but some peo]
were still urgent in their desire for (
expulsion of foreigners, and thus no deba
of any clan government ended with sad

factory results, so it was a very difficult matter to enter into final negotiations with the foreign Powers.

The Imperial Court was then called "Koke," and the Tokugawa Regency "Buke."

As they did not come to any agreement, the debates of all other clan governments ended without results. On seeing that the desire to expel foreigners was gaining ground both in Choshu and Satsuma, it was generally supposed that it was the desire of all Japan to expel them. In the meantime the Imperial power was restored, owing to the weakness of the Tokugawa Regency, which was the result of 300 years of peaceful tranquility in a dream of eternal peace and thus the "samurai" had lost all their former vigour and power; and at last the Shogun was obliged to go up to Kyoto, and hand over all power to the Emperor. By this time the feeling concerning the expulsion of foreigners had completely changed in favour of opening up the country.

Before the restoration our names were different. Kido was called Kogoro Katsura, Zoroku Murata was called Masujiro Omura, and I was named Uichi Hayashi. When I was called to the Imperial Court in the first year of Meiji, I was called Shunsuke Ito, so I did not change the name. Both at the restoration and in the Fushimi War, I was at home, because I intended to establish a school, where English should be taught, at Mitajiri, and an American followed me there, who wanted to be employed by me. I took him to Yamaguchi, and there I established a school. It was the 11th of January in the year of "Boshin" (1868) when I went again to Kobe. I was surprised to see that the town was filled with foreign forces while the people there were greatly excited. I had an interview with Parks, the British Minister, then went to Osaka where I had arranged preparations for declaring the "Restoration of the Imperial Power." Count Higashikuze was sent to Kobe in order to convey the Imperial Message to that effect, to the respective foreign Ministers, and thus the Restoration of the Imperial Power and the new Government was recognized by the Powers. As there was no system settled, I was temporarily appointed Secretary of Foreign Affairs. A month or tw afterwards the official system was settled and I was invested with the third degre of Chokunin Rank, being promoted to Judg of Foreign Affairs, and also appointe Governor of Osaka Fu. The supreme contr of the foreigners in Kobe was under m charge. In May of the same year the cla system was totally changed into a provincia one, and I was appointed Governor of Hyog Ken. Although I was the promoter of th new system, I experienced a difficulty i carrying it out, because neither the Imperia Court nor the clans had considered it s far. Wherever I went my opinion was re ceived with displeasure. Some "Shizoku ("samurai" before the Restoration) had then a vague expectation of being granted a large annual stipend each. So they did not agree with me, for fear they should lose their imaginary profit, in the event of the clan system being dispensed with. But, when I met Kido and expressed my opinion to him, I received his sympathy. I had still to prevail upon the Tosa and Higo clans, after doing so first with the Satsuma and Choshu clans. This I did with the valuable assistance of Princes Sanjo and Iwakura. I shall have to enlarge upon the circumstances, under which I obtained influence through both the Princes, and also about many other things which happened during the first year of the Meiji era (1868). Though

I fear I will repeat the same things several times, yet I will try my best to relate things in their proper order.

The first questions I shall dwell upon are finance and diplomacy. I was then appointed an officer in the Bureau of Budgets with the additional office of Judge. Then the Government system was changed according to the system which was in vogue in the epoch of Taiho. And as a result of this change, the Financial Department and Foreign Department were inaugurated. Count Okuma was then appointed Minister of the Financial Department, and I vice-Minister. During the term of my office I punished many persons who counterfaited the paper currency then issued.

At that time Count Okuma and I always worked together. We were planning how to introduce a railway system into this country, while studying out measures by which the Government might be able to keep up the value of the paper currency. We occupied ourselves in laying a railway between the Imperial Capital (Tokyo) and Yokohama from the 2nd year of Meiji (1869), and at length succeeded in this work, though we met almost insurmountable difficulties. As we, however, had had no studies in economical and budgetary questions, I had to go across to America for the purpose of investigating both, so I attended at the American Financial Office and studied both the subjects practically for half a year. Fukuchi, Yoshida, and Yoshikawa accompanied me on this journey. We were thus able to get a general idea about taxes, paper currency, income and expenditure, yearly budget, the system of national banks, superintending the Budget Office, Custom Houses, etc. I did not miss the opportunity of studying the American Constitution. When we came back to Japan I went to Osaka, where the Coinage Office was opened, and the business was placed on a gold standard, under the advice of the American Government. But after a while that standard fell into desuetude in this country. But in my first attempt I ordered gold coins to be minted, and then one yen silver coins as supplementary ones, after the style adopted by America. But by and by the gold coins disappeared from the market. At present, however, the gold standard is in force again to my great satisfaction.

Then the Cabinet was changed, and Okubo became the Lord of the Treasury; Inouye became Minister of Finance; and I became Chief of both the Tax and Coinage Offices, though it seemed that I was thus somewhat degraded in office. But it was necessary for the Cabinet that I should work in Osaka. Besides properly attending to my own official duties, I was then making all the provisions, regulations, and forms of the Financial Department. It was indeed very hard work for me. I called to my office paper manufacturers, and instructed them to make the paper which is now used in the Department in question. And thus I furnished the material with which Count Okuma was able to issue paper money at the Department. And afterwards we determined to establish national banks for giving protection to the value of the paper currency. I had national debt bonds prepared by Mr. Nakashima who had just come to America from Europe when I was coming back to Japan, and after a while Count Goto became the Minister of Industry; but he urgently asked me to take his place owing to his being incapable of performing the work of the office. Therefore I relieved him by appointment. Then Iwakura was ordered to visit Europe as our Plenipotentiary, but he did not wish to accept the appointment without my being among his party. So I was obliged to accompany him to foreign lands. Okubo and Kido wished to start on the same tour, so the party consisted of Iwakura, Kido, Okubo, some other secretaries, and myself. We left Japan in the winter of the 4th year of Meiji (1871), and spent the next year in Europe, returning in September of the 6th year of Meiji (1873).

When we returned, to our great surprise, hot debates arose in the Cabinet on the question of attacking Corea. Fortunately those who had once seen Europe objected to that bold enterprise on the ground that Japan should strive to be civilized within these twenty or thirty years as much as the foreign Powers, so that the Treasury could not afford great expenditures in order to gain a vain military reputation. Iwakura, Kido, and Okubo were very much interested in aiding the anti-war party, but without effect. And consequently the differences of their opinions caused dissension in the Cabinet. Following this event the Saga disturbance took place, and then Taiwan (Formosa) affair also disturbed our statesmen's minds. Regarding the Corean trouble, Okubo went across to China, and came back after settling the matter satisfactoriy to Japan. In the same year when he returned from China, Okubo presented me with a copy of the treatise on the forms of government written by him, for my reference library. Kido having retired from the Cabinet owing to his displeasure with the measure for attacking the peninsula, Okubo was then busily engaged in endeavouring to cause the cessation of the disquietude, while attending to the administration. So the Osaka Convention was held among us, Okubo, Kido, Inouye, Itagaki, and I; and there we freely exchanged opinions so that any misunderstanding should not upset the administrative organs. In April of the 8th year of Meiji (1875) a transformation was carried out regarding the administration. As a result of this the Supreme Court and the Senate House were inaugurated, and a meeting of all the Governors was held.

Thus the first foundation was laid for the constitutional government by the present Emperor. Before the proclamation of the Emperor regarding the constitutional government, I alone was mainly instrumental in furnishing the necessary documents, though Kido, Okubo, Itagaki, and I were all appointed as a committee. Afterwards the members of the Cabinet entertained different views as to whether the counselors should be divided from the other ministers of the respective Departments. Just then our man-of-war was fired at by the Coreans in the Kokwa Gulf (江華彎), and some members of the Cabinet proposed to chastize the Coreans, and to send our Plenipotentiary for the purpose, but the others objected.

At last Shimadzu and Itagaki resigned their offices, on account of the divisions in the Cabinet. So the rest of the members were obliged to form the Cabinet by themselves. Kuroda and Inouye were sent out to Corea to settle the Corean differences satisfactorily. In the 9th year of Meiji (1876) when the Emperor signified that it was his pleasure to travel through the northern provinces, Iwakura and Kido accompanied His Majesty, and Okubo, then Minister of State for Home Affairs, took the lead. His Majesty the Emperor and party proceeded to Awomori, whence they took a steamer back to the Palace. The Emperor wished to see Hokkaido, but was unable to do so from lack of time. On his return, Prince

Sanjo, Yamagata, Terajima, and I ordered to start on a journey to witness condition of the affairs in Hokkaido Akita, and we did so. On the way we heard of the Boxers of Kumamoto, we returned to the Imperial Capital great hurry. When we had put down Boxers, the Maibara affairs of Hagi place.

On the 31st of January in the year of Meiji (1877), the Anniversary the death of the late Emperor was hel Kyoto. This event necessitated the la of a railway between Kobe and K; At the time Emperor went to Kyoto railway was completed, and its inaugur ceremony was held. After the Annive ceremony was over, the Emperor visited the town of Kobe, on the 5th of February of that year, and on his way home to Tokyo, the rumour reached his ears that Saigo, of Kagoshima, had risen against the Imperial Court, and plundered the powder of the Government. So the Emperor proceeded to the Emperor Jimmu's grave to inform the Spirit of the dead Emperor of the matter, being accompanied by Prince Sanjo and Kido. In the meanwhile Yamagata and I stayed at Kobe. By and by the enemy became powerful. During the war Kido died, from natural causes. In the meantime connection was made between the Kumamoto Garrison and the Imperial army, and then the latter turned the day, and pursued the enemy towards the Hyuga province. And as it became easier to put them down, the Emperor returned to the Imperial Capital, being accompanied by us. In the spring of the next year when the rebellion was put down, a meeting of all the governors was held in Tokyo. At the time when the meeting was nearly finished, Okubo was assassinated. As his successor in office was not easily found, I was appointed Minister of State for Home Affairs.

The next question which followed this event was the fall of the value of the paper currency. Then Count Okuma proposed to float foreign bonds, while I was maintaining my opinion that we could get along by curtailing all the official expenses without adopting that measure. My opinion was at last adopted by the Emperor's orders in the 13th year of Meiji (1880). In the year following, Hokkaido was inspected by the authorities, and a Governor was sent to that island with the intention of encouraging the farming and fishing industries there. In the 23rd year of Meiji (1890), about nine years after that date, an Imperial edict was issued, declaring the Imperial Constitution to be in force. In preparing the steps for this I was sent to Europe again in the 15th year of Meiji (1882), and I studied there many subjects. First I met Prof. Gneist in Germany, and I received very valuable instruction from him. He was a professor of the Berlin University, and with him I discussed the English Constitution to my entire satisfaction. Afterwards I went to Australia, and there I studied the conditions under Dr. Stein. He was one of my principal instructors, and from him I gained much information, regarding diplomacy, political economy, naval and military affairs, justice and education, though I was taught in local administration by another instructor. During my studies of the subjects I copied his lecture on the state and its constitution, which he had touched upon philosophically, with the help of M. Ito, but I have unfortunately lost that copy.

To enter into the details of the second European tour, I have many experiences to ate. First of all I should like to divide the time into two parts: the period from the 1st year of Meiji (1868) to the 10th (1877); that is, the time of the restoration of the Imperial Power; from the 10th (1877) to the 22nd (1889); that is, the time of the preparation for constitutional government. As soon as the Imperial Government succeeded in putting down the Kagoshima rebellion the Government adopted the measure of encouraging discussion of political affairs among the people, the result of the meeting of all the Governors. The only difficulty which I experienced was the want of money in the treasury, because we had expended large sums both in suppressing the great rebellion,

and in making the necessary preparations f
the Constitutional Government.

As I knew exactly my superior
opinions regarding the Constitution
Government, I could not pass over the
without briefly touching upon them. A
I said before, in the winter of the 4th yea
of Meiji (1871), Iwakura, Udai Jin (cor
responding to Minister of State for Hom
Affairs); Okubo, Minister of State for th
Treasury, Kido, Councilor; Yamaguch
Minister of State for Foreign Affairs; an
myself were despatched to Europe as amba
sadors. The object of our being sent 1
foreign lands was to study their administr.
tions besides settling treaties with them
As you know, the European Powers we

almost all constitutionally governed countries. So the subjects we had to study were extensively arranged from constitutional actions down to both legislative and administrative affairs. Needless to say we had tried our best to bring back sound information as to those things. We returned home in the 6th year of Meiji (1873). Kido the Councilor then expressed his opinion to me that it was necessary for Japan that she should be constitutionally governed in the near future, in order to keep up the ship of State. I had the same opinion.

Regarding the "Restrition of the Imperial Power," I would simply say that it was easily done by the people being public-minded, of course putting aside their selfinterets; and furthermore, that the harmony between the ruler and the ruled was urgently desired by the whole nation in the hope that she might cope with the European Powers on the same footing. It is obvious that both the heavy tasks of the restration of the Imperial power, and of abolishing all the clans, and putting into force provincial systems instead, resulted from the people's earnest thirst for the betterment of the country. We then discussed the difficulty of making a new start for the change of government, so that our endeavours might end in one undivided object. Even Kido the Councilor expressed the same opinion about the difficulty.

The pamphlet, written by Okubo, that

states his opinion regarding constitutional government is still in my hands. It was written about the time when the question of attacking Corea arose. And after a while the different opinions on the measure in question resulted in the dissension of the Cabinet. Therefore Saigo and other councilors resigned their offices. After this event, the petition for electing members of the House of Commons was signed, and while the Government was planning how to adjust the administration. Many difficulties presented themselves, one following another, until the South-West Rebellion happened. About the time this was put down, all my superiors disappeared from the stage, owing either to *their deaths* from natural causes or to their being assassinated. Sanemitsu Sanjo remained on the stage and took the portfolio of Premier, Iwakura being appointed Udai Jin while Prince Arisugawa took charge of Sadai Jin (one of the Cabinet offices then in existence.) All the statesmen and politicians, with one accord, favoured the adoption of a constitution.

In the 14th year of Meiji (1881) Count Okuma tendered a petition to the Government to adopt it soon. But it, being a heavy task, was not easily adopted, because the question remained uncertain as to how to introduce the best form into this country. Each and every country is more or less different from any other in its government, though the final purpose is the same. Therefore the best form of government for one country is not sure to obtain the same results in another.

Though the question on this point had not yet been well studied, it was necessary to let the people know of the Government's decision previous to its being put into operation. An Imperial edict concerning it was issued in the same year (1881). At the same time I was ordered to go to Europe. The Imperial Message with which I was honoured was as follows:

"According to the Edict proclaimed by Us on the 12th day of the 10th month in the 14th year of Meiji (1881), We have strongly determined to make the new form of government complete and perfect, and already made due preparations, yet it is very important for Us to take the forms of the European Powers into Our consideration, before We shall adopt Our best one.

Therefore, We now send you to Europe where you may find men of profound knowledge, from whom you can learn exactly about the general structure of their governments, and all practical internal affairs. We confer upon you the position of Chief Secretary of the Extraordinary Plenipotentiary, and hope that you will well bear this heavy burden, and will come back in excellent health, without feeling any effects of fatigue.

The Imperial Signature.

3rd day of 3rd month in 15th year of

Ieiji.

Signed by Sanemitsu Sanjo, the Prenier, 1st degree of Rank and 1st degree of Merit."

The instructions annexed to the above edict were as follows:

1. Investigate exactly what is advantageous or otherwise, after studying about the origin and history of every constitutionally governed country.
2. Investigate the privileges of the royal families.
3. Investigate the properties of the royal family and of the princes or princesses of the blood.
4. Investigate the formation of a Cabinet, as well as the official rights

of the legislative, judicial, and diplomatic affairs.

5. Investigate the responsibility of a Cabinet.

6. Investigate the relations between the Houses of Lords and Houses of Commons.

7. Investigate the business of a Cabinet and its procedure.

8. Investigate the constructions of the Houses of Lords and House of Commons.

9. Investigate the system and privileges of the nobles.

10. Investigate the limitation of the official power of both Houses and their procedure.

Investigate the privileges of the royal family in both Houses.

Investigate the opening, dissolving, and adjourning of both Houses.

Investigate how free discussions be held in both Houses.

Investigate the dissensions regarding the privileges of both Houses.

Investigate the provisions regarding debates and discussions in the two Houses.

- Investigate the special rights of both Houses granted by the royal family.
- Investigate all the relations existing between the two Houses.
- Investigate where bills should be submitted as well as the manner of

introducing them.

19. Investigate the methods by whi decide the budget accounts, examine decisions.

20. Investigate the judicial rights of Houses.

21. Investigate petitions and the la administrative courts.

22. Investigate the requirements for returned as representatives of Houses, and the laws regarding tion.

23. Investigate the distinct limitati the rules and regulations of law administration.

24. Investigate the construction and of the respective Departments.

25. Investigate the several connections existing between the Houses and the respective Departments.

26. Investigate the connection between Governors and the respective Departments.

27. Investigate the ways of promoting and dismissing the Judicial officers.

28. Investigate the connection between the Judicial officers and the Houses.

29. Investigate the responsibility and general reasons for the resigning of all the officials.

30. Investigate the special favours and pensions granted to retired officials.

31. Investigate the local system of administration.

The above mentioned articles were t[he] main subjects upon which I must bri[ng] back information. So, when I left f[or] Europe, I carried with me a strong dete[r]mination to fulfil my duties. In Europe [I] acquired general information concernin[g] several forms of government now in vogu[e] in different countries there. In the 16t[h] year of Meiji (1883), I returned home fo[r] the purpose of starting my draft of th[e] proposed constitution of Japan. However, until the next year I could not do so, o[n] account of being too busy. It was just th[e] end of the 21st year of Meiji (1888), tha[t] I finished that work. On the 21st day [of] February of the 22nd year of Meiji (1889) the Imperial Constitution was at last issued after the Emperor's sanction had been given.

In the meantime the Privy Council Office was inaugurated for the purpose of disscussing questions regarding the constitution, and the provisions regarding the Imperial family law. Whenever the councilors were called together they were never without the presence of His Majesty the Emperor in the assembly-hall, though each meeting occupied a considerable space of time. And as often as I was taken in audience, the Emperor condescended to ask me many questions concerning the constitution, holding its draft in his hand. Thus our constitution was made under strict supervision of the Emperor, and was declared in the 22nd year of Meiji (1889).

In the winter of the year following the fi
Imperial Diet was convoked. Since t
event the new order of things has made
appearance up to date. I say, a period
from the 10th year of Meiji (1877)
the 22nd year of Meiji (1889) was sp
in making due preparations for adopting
constitutional government, and anoth
period of from the 22nd year of Me
(1889) till now [when the Marquis relat
this] was spent in its trial. In the mea
time I was appointed twice as Premier.
my own regret, however, I had to ta
recourse to such an extreme measure
dissolving the National Assembly e
time. Generally speaking, however,
Constitutional Government passed its

amination fairly well.

Before this, Prince Arisugawa was ordered to investigate several constitutions, when he was appointed President of the Senate. As a result of this a few constitutions of European Powers were translated into Japanese, and then all the senators were busily engaged in discussing which of them might be advantageously copied for our constitution. The mere translations were of little use. Besides those translations, I read many other books written in Japanese, on the same subject. But among them I could scarcely find any one worthy to be used as our reference-book, because most of them mainly dwelt upon the different views of many Cabinets, but nothing more. Thus all our endeavours having ended in failure, I was at last ordered to go to Europe for the purpose of making a thorough investigation of the same subject.

To tell the truth, this attempt of mine was exceedingly hard for me. In the event of George Washington's rendering his services for his country in adopting a constitution, those who rendered him assistance were great scholars such as James Madison, of Virginia, and Alexander Hamilton, of New York. In 1787, they published a book containing their own views regarding the constitution, in New York. That book is now kept in my library and tells me that they were indeed great scholars who nobly performed their duties for their country' sake. Though a republic is quite useful for a smaller country, yet there had been very few instances, in the world, of its being well suited for any large country. So it was very hard for them to adopt a republican form of government for their country; and I could not but highly praise their rare abilities for having done so, and to such good advantage. My attempt was quite the reverse of theirs, in method. Our constitution must be, in some way, based upon the popular rights; for the purpose of discussing administrative measures with the delegates of the whole nation, bills must be first submitted to the Diet. Though every European Constitution is well suited to its particular country, yet the limitation between popular rights and monarchical power is to ambiguous. So, my intention was to draw up a monarchical constitution for my country, in which provisions the limitation between the elements aforesaid should be distinctly defined and the rights of voting or of debating questions regarding the country's welfare and prosperity should be granted to the whole nation. To summarise; the American scholars in question made an effort to introduce a constitution for a popular republic, into their Continental Confederation, which system is applicable to a small country but not to a large one, as is proved by history. But I was making an endeavour to adopt a monarchical constitution for my country, despite the fact that a popular constitution was advantageous to European nations. The book written by them is called the Federalist, and contains their views on the American Constitution. When I went across to America for the purpose of investigating both the budget and economical questions, I took the opportunity of discussing the American Constitution with a few American scholars. In the meantime, I was informed, by them of this book which is very useful for studying the American Constitution. When I went again to Europe for the purpose of investigating all the affairs of several constitutionally governed countries, I gave all the powers of my mind to the study of history of constitutions, legality of constitutions, constitutionality, revision or disuse of constitutions, and many other subjects. I received information regarding such subjects as absolute sovereignty (which we see in the German monarchy), constitutional sovereignty, and constitutional popular rights, each of which I scrutinized afterwards. But on that visit I specially devoted both my time and labour to the study of constitutional sovereignty, in order that I might easily arrange materials for a proposed constitution of Japan. When I began to draw it up, I was very careful to make it harmonize as nearly as possible with our history. I was then assisted by M. Ito, K. Kaneko, and especially by K. Inouye. Among others who rendered me assistance that attempt there was a German by the name of Reusrel (?). He seemed to me a very learned man in economy and law, who had the affairs of the two countries, France and England, besides his own at his finger's ends. As often as we had difficult questions to solve before turning the draft into English, the great scholar very kindly gave us valuable suggestions. Afterwards we perused at once the original and translation very carefully, in order to make the draft free from blunders. And not having found any incongruous points legally between the two, we wrote it again in Japanese. From the 17th year of Meiji (1884) I was daily occupied in studying the proposed attempt, while giving attention to the administration of the country. And furthermore I had to draw up the regulations of the Imperial family, the law of election, and that of the two Houses. Seeing that almost all my attempts were coming to a successful end, I resigned my portfolio of Premier in the 5th month of the 21st year of Meiji (1888). Afterwards Privy Councilors were first nominated, of whom I was President. Discussions and debates were repeated many times before the sittings of all the Councilors, before the Imperial sanction was granted to the constitution, and you may well imagine what a hot debates we three, K. Inouye, M. Ito, K. Kaneko and I, were engaged in on the eve of the formal *Declaration*, which was celebrated on Kigeneetsu Festival; that is the 11th day of the 1st month of the 22nd year of Meiji (1889). Though I had my own opinion as to how to prescribe every provision of the Constitution, yet it was impossible to follow my own judgment; because evidently the supreme power belongs to His Majesty the Emperor. Hence I could do nothing with it, and there were evident difficulties in regard to the provisions of budget, justice, and both the Houses. If I am not mistaken, it was in March of the 15th year of Meiji (1882) that I went across to Europe for the purpose of determining which form of government would be best adapted to this country; and it was in August of the 16th year of Meiji (1883) that I returned from the investigation tour.

In or about March or April of the same yea
the Coronation Ceremony of the Czar w
expected to be held at Moscow, and Princ
Arisugawa (senior) was sent there as Envo
Extraordinary. The Prince, however, re
turned owing to the ceremony's having bee
postponed till May or June of the same yea
As I was then in Europe I was ordered t
attend the grand ceremony, in lieu of th
Prince. So, on the way home I went t
Moscow to represent Japan. As I hav
spoken at considerable length on the makin
of our constitution, let me now relate som
thing on the political affairs of those day
In the 16th year of Meiji (1883), I w
appointed President of the Privy Counci
in the spring of the next year Minister

State for the Imperial Household, with the former office. During my term in office I experienced an almost insurmountable difficulty in executing a thorough change for the Imperial Household, in accordance with the provisions of the Imperial Constitution. To my own regret, I say Prince Iwakura, one of my predecessors, being once numbered could not see the new order of things coming in. In the same year (1884), Corean trouble with Corea occurred, and consequently there arose in the Cabinet different views as to whether or not Japan should send an expedition to Corea. Then I ventured my honour in settling the trouble in question, though it was thought a heavy task by all. In the spring of the 18th year of Meiji (1885) I went across to China for the purpose, having the capacity of Minister of State for the Imperial Household. When I came back from China, I was nearly overwhelmed with many heavy tasks; because I had to draw up our constitution, while bearing the responsibility of bringing the Corean trouble to a successful issue, besides investigating many other things such as the administrative affairs as well as the local system and political questions. The above investigations being finished I had still to turn them to provisions so that they might be put into operation. At the end of the same year (1885), I formed a Ministry by command of the Emperor. The greatest change that I had executed through every organ of administration should be regarded merely as a preparation for putting the Constitution into operation. Previous to the "Declaration of the Imperial Constitution," many memorable events took place, one following another. The most noticeable ones among them were the Corean trouble, and the attempt at revising the treaties with the Powers, which was broken off abruptly, owing to Count Okuma's being shot by a so-called "soshi" (one of the followers belonging to a politician). At the time when the revised treaties were being negotiated by the Count I resigned my portfolio, for reasons which it is not necessary to mention here. I was, however, ordered by the Emperor to attend the meetings of the Cabinet in the capacity of President of the Privy Council. But in October of the 22nd year of Meiji (1889), I declined this, too. In the meanwhile the Cabinet being broken up, Prince Sanjo temporarily took up the ship of the State. In the 23rd year of Meiji (1890), Yamagata became Prime Minister, and at the end of the year the National Diet was convoked. Till that time I was still President of the Privy Council, but I resigned at the close of the session. As the next Ministry was not readily formed by any statesman, I was ordered by the Emperor to stand as Premier, but even then I was unable to consent.

[When the Marquis declined to take up *the task* of forming the next Cabinet, we are told, the Emperor had signified his pleasure to the effect that the Marquis' services would be urgently required in case the country might be in danger; and then the Marquis taking it to heart with much feeling retired from the Imperial presence. Was it not a strange coincidence that the Marquis stood up bravely to form a Cabinet, when the Japan-China War broke out and the country rushed into a probable danger? No wonder, he was invested with the peerage as a Marquis and also decorated with the Order of the Grand Cordon, in recognition of his meritorious deeds during the war. We think, however, that his valuable services in drafting a constitution for Japan ranks first of all his meritorious

' deeds. The translator is now very muc[h] pleased to introduce the Marquis' opinion o[f] the Constitution.]

[Before proceeding to my subject, le[t] me relate things somewhat in order. Though there are many opinions regarding a constitution, let me first dwell upon what the Japanese Constitution is. Some scholars have had a conception that there are two sources from which the supreme power is derived. To them, I must say a few words as to the basis upon which the Japanese Constitution stands. Some Japanese scholars of the Chinese classics adhering to the opinion that any living creatures in the domain of the Emperor must be absolutely his own subjects, entertain some fears coning the present Constitution. So, I k that it is my duty to let them have tisfactory explanation. I will briefly k as to [why the Imperial supreme power unlimitted in appointing his servants,] political parties are necessary for the ntry, and the responsibility of the two res.

According to the present scholars who fess constitutional law as their speciality, re are two kinds of constitutions; the being unchangeable, and the other ngeable. Fears are entertained, that understanding may be found among tical parties, unless they know of this ory. [In the unchangeable Constitu i, the supreme power, popular rights, construction of the National Diet, and the official powers of the Treasury and Justice are clearly prescribed by laws, so that any intrenchment of rights shall not occur, and such is found to be the Japanese Constitution. The changeable constitution is such as we find in England, which can be altered according to the requirements of each epoch. You see, the English Constitution has undergone marvelous changes in accordance with the necessities of each period, say from the XII century down to the XIX century. In technical terms, we call the latter a flexible constitution, and the former a rigid one. In short, that which is historically constituted is a flexible one, and that which has resulted from a llision between a Sovereign's power and is subjects' is the one that we call a rigid onstitution. The French Constitution is in outcome of the internal disorder of the country. There the tyranical government of the Emperors and the arbitary acts of both the priests and nobles excited the unchangeable fire of national wrath, so much so that the cry of establishing the popular rights became louder and louder till it eventually turned into the French Revolution, by which the people destroyed the supreme power of the Royal family and successfully adopted the popular constitution, based upon the opinion of Montesquieu, and others.

There exists, however, no such analogy n the history of our constitution, as we have seen in that of the French Constitution. Though there once arose some powerful political parties favouring the popular rights before our constitution was adopted, yet [I can say, without any fear of contradiction, that the Japanese Constitution differs greatly from that made under the heavy pressure of the people of France.] I wish I could draw the attention of our politicians of to-day to this point, that the circumstance which necessitated making our constitution is quite different from that of a foreign country. [The latter has generally resulted from a collision between the ruler and the ruled, while the former was made with one accord between the Emperor and the people in order to protect and to promote the national interests and welfare with a combination of all the existing powers. I was surprised to see that some politicians or scholars of this country were going to study some European Constitutions so as to easily understand ours, because I thought it not worth while to do so. I remember that a petition to adopt a constitutional government was submitted to the Throne. But I doubt whether or not that man understood constitutional politics. Nay, it is quite absurd to imagine that there were many Japanese who fairly understood the European Constitutions. It was of course necessary for Japan to decide her form of government, at that time. Yet the purpose and circumstance of the making of our constitution were quite different from those of the making of European Constitutions. When the Shogunate's authority was falling to the ground, the restoration of the Imperial power was at work, and at last succeeded. Because, seeing the requirements of the day the whole nation united in order that she could enter into a competitive struggle with foreign Powers. This was the reason why the military and financial powers were so nicely combined. To tell the truth, however, those who had been dreaming of the feudal system which lasted some seven hundred years, seemed not to be aware that the system should be entirely abolished, till it became too late. Even those scholars who were in favour of the restration of the Imperial political supremacy did not dream that the system should be entirely dispensed with, because they thougt that it was a suitable system for Japan. And I have an authority to prove that idea of theirs. [It was he that first laid a foundation of the feudal system, when the Emperor Jimmu, the Founder of the Empire, started on an eastern expedition to subdue all the insurgents in Eastern Japan and returned with a glorious victory to the Palace at Yamato. Since then every province was governed by its hereditary Lord called Kunitsukasa (chief of a province), and this way of administration continued for a considerable period, until it was *thoroughly reformed* by the Emperor Tenchi, who had newly appointed Governors revokable at his pleasure, instead of the hereditary Lords. This was the first instance in which the Emperor and the subjects were placed in a closer connection. Whereas such a vicissitude as this is shown by history, my lack of time does not allow me to dwell fully upon it here. Since a monarchical form of government was laid by the Emperor in question, the Fujiwara family (the coart nobles), who monopolized the privilege of getting near the persons of the August Masters, became naturally empowered, and in consequence of it the Imperial power lost its true lustre. Unhappily it came to pass that all the provinces of this country were filled up with robbers or freebooters, by whom the peace of the country was nearly destroyed As the court nobles became then effeminate, the Emperors were obliged to depend upon the military forces of the two families, the Minamoto and the Taira, by necessity, in order to put down the freebooters of the country. In the meantime, the two families becoming equal in power became jealous of each other, and after a long doubtful battle the latter eventually lost its day and was deplorably ruined, while the former became so powerful that they established a feudal government at Kamakura, which was the origin of the Shogunate Government. Seeing that such a double governments could not respond to the requirements of the

State, the nation abolished the Shogunate Government with its feudal lords, and the Imperial Government alone came in force.]

Since this revolution we have had no more political elements in the Empire than the Emperor and his subjects, though we had had more than two in the pre-restoration days. Then nothing was more necessary for the country than prescribing the Imperial political supremacy as well as adopting a stable form of government. As far as theories are concerned, administration has no function, unless the action of the political supremacy is defined, because administration is nothing but connecting the relation between the ruler and the ruled. On the part of the former, nothing is mo cessary than letting the latter satisfy with ministering good laws. To do this the rmer must provide a stable constitution or the latter. I say the Japanese Con- ⟵ titution is not an outcome of any conflict between the Emperor and his people, but a nice harmony of the two political elements did tend to bring it in. This tendency must arrest the attention of the outsiders of politics as well. I regret to say, however, that some of our politicians have carelessly overlooked it and fallen into an erroneous interpretation of our constitution. Not only do I earnestly hope that the present constitution will last forever, but I feel it to e the greatest responsibility of mine to and by it with vigilance during my life, owing to my having been instrumental in drawing it up. So, if any scholars or politicians of profound knowledge speak against the principle of our constitution, I, who abide as the cause of it, shall never yield myself from the ground.

Our constitution, being a rigid one, can not be altered, unless the Emperor's proposal be first heard and united by the decision of the two Houses. The reason why ours is different from the European Constitutions is this, that the political supremacy is possessed by the Emperor, in this country, while the definition that the supreme authority is in possession of the people gave rise to the popular constitutions which are in vogue in some parts of Europe. Ac ording to the constitutions that copied the Popular Constitution of France, the supreme power belongs to the people On the contrary the German Constitution defines the supreme power as being in possession of the Emperor. But it being made during the period from 1848 to 1853, the general feature of it seems to be somewhat influenced by the excitement of the people infected with the political inflamation that attacked France. So, the question where the supreme power exists solves a difference of governments and administrations. Assuming that the political supremacy rests on the side of a people we will arrive at this conclusion that the people can alter or dispense with their Sovereign at their own

pleasure. But such an opinion can
be admitted in such a country as J
Though the people have cried for l
or popular rights, yet, I am sure, a
them can not be induced to favour
an opinion as moving the Emperor at
pleasure. Even though there are now
Sovereigns in the constitutionally gov
countries of Europe, if they can be n
at the peoples' pleasure those governi
are republics in substance, no matter
they are called. On the contrary, tha
supreme power remains in the hands
August Master involves the principle
the Sovereign is too sacred to be mov
the people's pleasure. I say our h
lling which of the two principles is

suited for Japan, is a good spokesman for me. We have called our Emperor "Tenshi Sama" which, literally translated, means "Heaven's Son," and this is also a signification that he enjoys the so-called omnipotent power on earth. But when our Emperors lived in Kyoto, they kept the mere title "Tenshi Sama," while the Shogunates ruled over the country. Seeing that perverted order of affairs the nation cried out and carried out "the restoration of the Imperial power." Nothing is meant by the phraseology but that the political supremacy is restored to the present Emperor. This is also an authentic reason why there is a great difference between the European Constitutions and ours.

Well, let me speak my opinion from a European point of view. According to the European scholars who presume that the supreme power rests on the side of a Sovereign, he can trust any of his subjects for the operation of his supremacy. Such a Sovereign can give certain rights to his people, though the supreme power is only one and can not be divided. But according to Montesquieu and Rousseau, the supreme power is divisible, though their opinion is now ignored by most of the present scholars. According to Montesquieu again, the legislature must be independent, though there is its organ, namely a diet, and even justice and administration must be also independent. There lurks a great mistake in his plausibl oning, that a government must have ee independent organs; because it is dent that a great misfortune would ur, were the departments to differ in nion. No wonder the truth that the reme power is indivisible is widely adtted by the jurists of to-day. [Therefore, e so-called supremacy must be the unnitted power that permanently remains in e hands of a Sovereign.] Though this is livisible, yet its functions may be enforced means of capable men. The legislature established for the purpose of letting the ~~eple~~ take part in enacting law, [that is to , of letting the people take part in emying the supreme power of the Emperor.] u see, the members of the two Houses being duly empowered by virtue of t[he] Emperor's supremacy, can discuss ma[ny] questions of great import for the countr[y]. As to both administration and justice, t[he] same reasoning holds good. Well, suc[h] rights given by the Emperor may be take[n] back by him at any time. However, su[ch] an extreme measure should not be tak[en] by him without an ample reason, as manifested in the constitution. As I ha[ve] so minutely touched upon the reason a[nd] circumstance of the two opinions, viewi[ng] the supreme power in different ways, [I] believe that any body must be satisfied wi[th] this explanation.

Now, let me here point out the m[is]conception cherished by the scholars

Chinese classics in this country. They, in nine cases out of ten, ignore the things which do not agree with the principle of an absolute monarchy, owing to their misconception that the very new order of things will spoil the national honour. Their fundamental idea is that each and every piece of ground of the Empire as well as each and every creature living in it must be absolutely his. No wonder, therefore, the present constitution was reflected to their eyes, as if it were a stumbling block lying in the way of our national growth. That they still stick to their old dogma is not because they are illiterate, but because they are so narrow-minded that they would not study ancient and modern politics as well as the substances. At once admittin[g] their opinion and supposing the Empero[r] should act imprudently, for example i[n] giving a certain district of land to th[e] people and soon taking it back from the[m] how can the people stand such an arbitar[y] act? It is quite needless to say. At a[ny] rate, a constitutional government is differe[nt] from a monarchical one in the followi[ng] point. Under the constitutional governme[nt] each person can not go beyond the prop[er] sphere of his own rights, at the same time h[is] estates and life can be well protected by t[he] law of the State. If there is an irration[al] government quite reverse from the abo[ve] condition of affairs, we call it a monachi[c] or rather tyrannical government. I shall f[

ther proceed to prove that what I have said is right. In Europe the position of a Sovereign and his power are understood as follows;—

When one country negotiates with another, the relation is the same as if a man deals with another, because each country is represented by its Sovereign. However, the phrase "to represent" does not convey any proper meaning of the conditions in Japan. So, in such a case I would rather say that our Emperor manifests Japan, though in Europe the phrase finds its proper use because in such a case European nations think as if the area of a country as well as its population were put together into a bag. In employing the word "to manifest," I am sure, we can clearly indicate to foreign ers the principle that each and every piece of ground in the Empire as well as each and every creature in it must belong to him absolutely. In Japan, making a de claration of war or peace as well as entering into a treaty with a foreign country are performed by the Emperor's supremacy, so that from that date the nation may enjoy the rights obtained by virtue of the treaty entered into, and at the same time must bear the responsibility caused by it, with out requiring any function of law. I think that the principle cherished by the scholar of Chinese classics is thus made clear. Though our constitution is written in plain language, yet I have often listened to some misleading lectures given upon the subject in class-rooms. The teachers' having made mistakes is not on account of their shallow knowledge, but because of their being careless concerning the two points, of which I have already dwelt upon. Generally speaking, our constitution can be easily understood by all, though not without a few exceptions, on account of its being written in plain and clear sentences.

And then let me say a few words on the political parties. So far as my opinion goes, they are those groups of men who differ from one another in political points of view. That human beings are naturally "political animals" is often said by the European scholars, and I think that is true, because we form ourselves into society, and live as much as we do at home, and are governed by the ruler by whom our lives and properties are equally protected. This is why we, the Soul of all creatures, are different from the droves of sheep, cows, and horses. We first form ourselves into society and then into a nation. We make homes, villages, cities, and eventually a state. Is there any animal that can make a state? No, there is really none except the Soul of all creatures. The epithet "political animals" is well said of human beings. It is evident that several political parties should have different points of view, when a country enters into negotiation with another, or when several important questions arise, such political or economical questions. A group of men who have the same opinion in politics is called a political party. Therefore, those who do not belong to any party seem to me a party called "non-political," because there are no persons in Japan who have no views on politics, whether they belong to a party or not. So, we need not put too much stress upon the so-called political parties, because we were all born "political animals." Suffice it to regard them as groups of men who represent the different opinions of the nation. But our political parties being yet young in growth, I am sorry to mention that they have thought it their duty to fight with each other in the Diet, as the Minamoto and the

Taira family as well as the Nitta and Ashikaga fought in the ancient times. I think such is an unpardonable misunderstanding, and I can not see the reason why they are strenuously competing to gain political ascendency. Physically speaking, they are merely instruments to represent different opinions of the people at the Diet. When a party-Cabinet is formed under the Imperial confidence, it must of course undertake the responsibility of administering impartially, as the spring rain comes down on all green things. On the contrary, if the Cabinet act injudiciously and favour their own party in administering, such is indeed a great hindrance to the national progress So, I earnestly hope such a misunderstanding will not occur in future.

To prevent such a mishap, the growth of many more political parties is indeed a desirable thing. The nation must have different opinions on politics, and as it is quite impossible to go round and ask each person's view, each party must have its own opinion decided before the session is convoked. Seeing that a political party has formed a Cabinet, some government officials are said to have spoken against the provision of the present constitution, stating that " those who belong to a political party can not become officials," as if they have found an incongruity in it. But I think this is also a mistake, and I may safely say that the Emperor can appoint any persons, no

matter whether they belong to a polit[ical]
party or not, because our Emperor is an [im]partial being, and has no prejudices. If [it]
be not true, the supremacy will be restri[cted,]
but we must remember that it is too sacr[ed to]
be interfered with. If there be any pol[itical]
party which dare act arbitarily we shal[l not]
hesitate to call them rebels, as much as [Yori]tomo Minamoto who started the Shog[un]
Government at Kamakura, without an[y Im]perial sanction. If the Emperor appoint[s this]
man or that to the highest office, it is no[t for]
the people to gainsay, because it is do[ne by]
his political supremacy. I say, each [and]
every Japanese enjoys the right to becom[e an]
official as well as many other rights preco[nized]
in the present constitution. It is, how[ever]

—[143]—

necessary for the people to have due qualifications, if they wish to become officials, because it is evident that all government officials must be educated men. The urgent requirement of to-day is to educate young men, and to consolidate the national foundation by means of a progressive form of government, and to promote the national wealth. In order to accomplish the latter end, we must depend mainly upon the polytechnic and scientific education. It is obvious that farming must be improved by agricultural science, machinery by the science of engineering, commerce by commercial science. It is needless to say that scientific knowledge should go hand in hand with practice. As all undertakings should be properly conducted and speedily improved by means of scientific knowledge, followed by practice, it is evident that those officers who stand before the people should be men who have due qualifications. The provision of the present constitution, stating that "any person who wishes to become an officer must have due qualifications," involves the possibility of any person becoming an officer. Seeing that the people now enjoy the freedom of religious belief such as Christianity, Shintonism, Buddhism and the like, we can safely arrive at the conclusion that those who belong to political parties may no doubt be appointed officers, as the Emperor is impartial to all. Such is not only my *opinion*, but all who wish to see the prosperity of the present constitution must have the same conviction.

Let me now dwell upon the National Diet. The representatives being returned from different political parties, they deem themselves something like rivals met together. The diet is not the place where a gladiatorial contest is held; no, indeed! They are called together in order that they may discuss political questions for the nation and arrive at the best solutions; that is to say, if this measure is beneficial for the people in general or if that one is pernicious. Sometimes there comes a question of increasing taxes. Then it is unavoidable that one part of the nation should be sacrificed in the interest of the general happiness of the whole. In employing reciprocal measures, a balance shoul[d] taken by the statesmen for administ[ering] laws. Thus it is evident that diff[erent] political parties must always take an [im]partial view of matters. However, I often witnessed that different parties in the Diet fought with each other, a volley of sneering words, as if they discovered in the National Diet a good [place] for revenge. I can not but reproach [the] foolish act of the representatives, becau[se it] will defame the history of the State.

The question following is that of responsibility of the two houses. "The system of the two Houses was w[ell ad]ed to this country is now admitte[d but] scholars and by those who favour popular rights, though there was once a time when the system of one House was highly recommended. The only defect of the system of a symple House is that any hasty and imperfect measures once decided upon in questions of much import, such as the budget or any other question, can not be altered, and in consequence of this the nation must sustain an injury. That it is much more advisable to discuss the same question more than once, is the main reason for the system of two Houses being introduced into Japan. So, I hope that the two Houses will go hand in hand harmoniously discarding all petty private differences. On the contrary, if they deem it

their pleasure to avenge each other in tl
Diet, they are indeed forgetting the
responsibility. This year an attempt w
made to revise the election law in ord
that both the industrial and commerci
classes might have their due share of in
terests in the National Assembly. But th
proposal ended in failure, on account of th
House of Lords not having given consen
This indicates that, unfortunately, the tv
Houses were not on good terms.

For fear such a mishap may recur,
dare repeat that the two Houses must
quite harmonious for the country's sak
sacrificing each and every private intere
for the welfare of the nation. At tl
same time I hope wise political parties w

grow in number, by necessity. As the Emperor possessing the political supremacy is quite free to appoint any person to the highest office under him; so, if a politician becomes a Premier, he can unscrupulously form his Cabinet with his own party. In the event of the party-Cabinet being taken into confidence by the Emperor, who is generous and impartial to the whole nation, they must respond to the responsibility, doing their best in ruling the nation at once impartially and beneficially. In concluding this appeal, let me repeat my wish that the present constitution may continue forever and that our political parties may conscientiously meet their responsibility in bettering the condition of our country.

1.

NAGASAKI,

DIRECTIONS

AS TO

PRIVATE LESSONS IN JAPANESE

AND ENGLISH,

BANKS, SHOPS,

BAZAARS, ADVOCATES,

PHOTO-ARTISTS, ETC.

OWARICHO, TOKYO, MAIN OFFICE.

OGAWAMACHI, HIROSHIMA,
NAGASAKI, "TENSHODO FIRM" YOKOHAMA,
OSAKA, KINGORO EZAWA, PROP'R. OTARU.

Importer, Manufacturer, and, Dealer in Diamonds, Watches, Clocks, Graphones, Bicycles, Jewelry, Optical Goods, Artistic Productions in Precious metals and Stones, and Rifles.

GRAND PRIZE, PARIS, 1900.

No. 40, IMAKAJIYA-MACHI,
NAGASAKI, JAPAN.   TELEPHONE: NO. 229.
CABLE ADDRESS:— "TENSHODO, NAGASAKI!"

テンシヨドウ　チヤジシカマイキサガナ

S. FUTAYEDA,

DEALER

IN

EMBROIDERY, TORTOISE—SHELL AND IVORY WORKS,

No. 85, *HIGASHI-HAMANO-MACHI*,

NAGASAKI, JAPAN.

BEST WORMANSHIP, LATEST FASHION, AND FANCY DESIGNS.

The Futayeda Shoten (firm) has been awarded Medals, Prizes and cerficates of Merit at EXPOSITIONS HOME and ABROAD.

The Futayeda Shoten (firm) is located in the central part of the city, and every possible attention is given to orders from Ladies and Gentlemen.

長崎東濱町八十五番地
二枝鼈甲店
ハマノマ チ フ タ エ ダ

The Nagasaki Branch
OF
Mitsui Ginko,
UNLIMITED,
NO. 72, NISHIHAMANO-MACHI,
NAGASAKI, JAPAN.

Manager.....................Y. TAN.
HAID UP CAPITAL............Yen 5,000,000.
RESERVED FUND............Yen 5,600,000.

Interest Allowed on Fixed Deposits.

For 1 Year 5.5% per annum.

For 6 months and upwards 5%.

On Current Account at .7 sen per 100 yen on Daily Balance.

On Petty Current Account at 1 sen per 100 *yen* on Daily Balance.

For Deposit at Notice the rate of interest will be given on application.

長崎市西濱町七十二番 三井銀行支店

"ISHIMARU SHOTEN,"

ヒガシハマノマチ
イシマル商店

(石)

DEALER
IN (One price only.)
STATIONERY,
NO. 18, HIGASHIHAMANO-MACHI,
NAGASAKI, JAPAN.
(TELEPHONE: No. 601.)

文房具商

THE "JAPAN HOTEL,"

長崎市大浦二十五
ジヤパンホテ"

25, OURA, NAGASAKI, JAPAN.
TELEPHONE: NO. 664.
Telegraphic Address: "JAPAN HOTEL."
ABC Code Used.

Good and healthy locality, five minutes' w[alk] from the landing stages. First-class acc[om]modation, especially for families. Excellent Fr[ench] Cuisine. A new separate House, from which [a] beautiful view of the surrounding country [can] be obtained, the House being wafted by the [cool] North-east breezes. Comfort and Satisfactio[n].

TERMS MODERATE.

Special rates to families and others for [a] prolonged stay.

SHINTARO SHIMIDZU,
Proprietor and Manager.

PHOTO-ARTIST.

Enlarginig, Reproducing, and
Out-door Work.
Japanese Costumes for Portraits
on Hand.
Work done for Amateurs.
Views and Albums for sale.
Charges moderate.
Orders promptly executed.

TENYOKWAN,

NO. 41, MOTOSHIKKUI-MACHI,
NAGASAKI, JAPAN.
(OPPOSITE BAZAAR)

長崎モトシックイマチ四十一 テンヨークワン

SAKATA & CO,

MANUFACTURERS

OF

TORTOISE-SHELL WARE.

Prices moderate. Orders promptly executed.

MOTOKAGO-MACHI,
NAGASAKI, JAPAN.
(TELEPHONE; No. 912.)

ナガサキレモトカゴマチ

OWARICHO, TOKYO, MAIN OFFICE.

OGAWAMACHI, HIROSHIMA,
NAGASAKI, "TENSHODO FIRM" YOKOHAMA,
OSAKA, KINGORO EZAWA, PROP'R. OTARU,

Importer, Manufacturer, and, Dealer in Diamonds, Watches, Clocks, Graphones, Bicycles, Jewelry, Optical Goods, Artistic Productions in Precious metals and Stones, and Rifles.

GRAND PRIZE, PARIS, 1900.

No. 40, IMAKAJIYA-MACHI, TELEPHONE: No. 229.
NAGASAKI, JAPAN.
CABLE ADDRESS:— "TENSHODO, NAGASAKI."

テンシヨドウ　チヤマジカマイキサガナ

舶來雑貨
毛織物類
洋酒問屋

長崎市東濱町本通り
村山商店
電話四百六十二番

GENTS' FURNISHING GO(
White and Crepe Shirts, Collars, Cuff[s
nekcties, Collar Buttons, Cuff Links,
and Tie Clips.
Whole sale dealers in Foreign Spirits
Woolen Stuffs.

MURAYAMA &

HIGASHI-HAMANO-MACHI,
NAGASAKI, JAP
(TELEPHONE: No. 462.)

西洋くわし
せいぞうしよ
清洋

長崎市にしはまのまち

THE SEIYOTEI

CONTRACTORS OF PROVISI
FOR
The Imperial Navy.

Manufacturers of all kinds of Candies, Ca[
Dainties in European and American S
68, NISHIHAMANO-MACHI,
NAGASAKI, JA
MANAGER................ICHIJI YA
(*Telephone:* No. 221.)

LAW OFFICE.

T. ISHIBASHI, ADVOCATE, B. L

EVERY class of Legal work undertaken and carried out promptly in Confidence. Special attention given to Commercial Cases. Compromises and Arbitrations arranged.

CHAMBERS,
No. 41, *TOGIYAMACHI*,

Nagasaki, Japan.

(TELEPHONE: No. 830.)

法學士 辯護士 石橋友吉法律事務所
長崎市磨屋町四十一番
イシバシトモキチホウリツジムショ

TASHIRO & Co.,

No. 14, Funadaiku-machi,

NAGASAKI, JAPAN.

TRADE (T) MARK.

FINE ART CURIOS,
IVORY WARES, PICTURES, CLOISONNE
EARTHEN WARES, EMBROIDERIES, ETC
ALL GOODS GUARANTEED.

Prices moderate. Orders promptly executed.

美術雜貨 陶磁器亙反賣 田代商店
長崎市船大工町十四番地
タシロシヨウテン

"SENOO SHOTEN,"
DEALER IN PHOTOGRAPHIC MATERIALS,
HIGASHI-HAMANO-MACHI,

NAGASAKI, JAPAN.

Telephone: No. 802.

ヒガシハマノマチ

(シヤシンキカイアリマス)

ONE PRICE ONLY.
ORDERS PROMPTLY EXECUTED.

"LESSONS in ENGLISH."

"LESSONS in JAPANESE."

THE WRITER OF THE PRESENT BOOK, with the highest credentials, is prepared to give lessons in ENGLISH and JAPANESE.

Adress J. Kuramata,

NO. 25, UMA-MACHI,
NAGASAKI, JAPAN.

WS - #0103 - 230123 - C0 - 229/152/10 - PB - 9780282594725 - Gloss Lamination